D0056535

# CONTEMPORARY LIVES

# JAY-Z

## HIP-HOP MOGUL

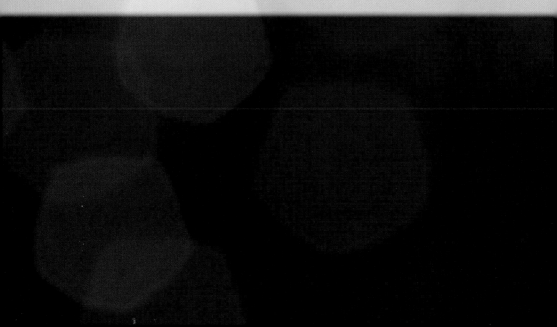

**ABDO**
Publishing Company

# CONTEMPORARY LIVES

# JAY-Z

## HIP-HOP MOGUL

by Paul Hoblin

# CREDITS

Published by ABDO Publishing Company, PO Box 398166,
Minneapolis, MN 55439. Copyright © 2012 by Abdo Consulting
Group, Inc. International copyrights reserved in all countries.
No part of this book may be reproduced in any form without
written permission from the publisher. The Essential Library™ is a
trademark and logo of ABDO Publishing Company.

Printed in the United States of America,
North Mankato, Minnesota
112011
012012

 THIS BOOK CONTAINS AT LEAST 10% RECYCLED MATERIALS.

Editor: Holly Saari
Copy Editor: Amy Van Zee
Series design and cover production: Emily Love
Interior production: Kelsey Oseid

**Library of Congress Cataloging-in-Publication Data**
Hoblin, Paul.
 Jay-Z : hip-hop mogul / by Paul Hoblin.
    p. cm. -- (Contemporary lives)
 Includes bibliographical references and index.
 ISBN 978-1-61783-325-0
 1. Jay-Z, 1969---Juvenile literature. 2.  Rap musicians--United
States--Biography--Juvenile literature. I. Title.
 ML3930.J38H63 2012
 782.421649092--dc23
 [B]
                                    2011040470

# TABLE OF CONTENTS

New Yorker Jay-Z is a well-known Yankees fan. He even performed before one of their World Series games in 2009.

## CHAPTER 1

# Famous
# New Yorker

n November 6, 2009, New York City threw itself a party. Confetti rained; rolls of toilet paper unraveled. The day before, the New York Yankees had won Major League Baseball's World Series. More than 3 million fans now lined the streets of the city to celebrate. Those in the office buildings above the streets lined up at the glass windows to watch the parade below. Many of those celebrating were lifelong Yankees fans. They had watched their team win other World Series titles, but that didn't diminish their excitement about this championship. It had been nine years since the Yankees had been major league champions, and people began lining the streets at 5:00 a.m. to welcome their return.

When the much-loved Yankee captain appeared, the crowds chanted "De-rek Je-ter! De-rek Je-ter!"[1] And as World Series Most Valuable Player (MVP) Hideki Matsui's float went by, another chant erupted: "MVP! MVP! MVP!"[2] The Yankee players stood on floats that wound their way along a stretch of Broadway called the Canyon of Heroes.

The players kept coming, and the fans kept cheering. But then, suddenly, many of the fans stopped. Instead of lifting their voices, they lifted

## HIGH EXPECTATIONS

The Yankees have won 27 World Series titles in their history, which is the most by far of any major league baseball team. For most teams, nine years between World Series titles doesn't seem very long. Several teams have never won a World Series. Still, Yankees fans expect their team to win the title every season.

The hand signal Jay-Z makes is called the "Diamond Cutter." He originally used the symbol as a sign of confidence and success. He and his buddies flashed the symbol when discussing an album that his record company, Roc-A-Fella Records, represented. They claimed the album was going to go diamond.

their arms. They touched their fingertips together, forming a diamond. By this time, most of the fans knew the meaning of that hand signal. It stood for Roc-A-Fella Records, the company that began by selling hip-hop music and then branched out to clothing and much more. Roc-A-Fella was founded by three people, including rapper and business mogul Jay-Z. When the diamond signal reached to the sky, Jay-Z was often near.

|||||||||||||||||||||||||||||||||||||||||||||||||||||||||||

## JAY-Z APPEARS

Sure enough, there he was, standing on a float next to all-star third baseman Alex Rodriguez. The rapper was decked out in Yankees gear: a black jacket with white stripes on the cuffs and waistband and a black hat with *NY* sewn on the front. His appearance was unannounced but not unexpected. Jay-Z is a lifelong New Yorker and has become one of the most well-known Yankees fans in the world. As he stood on that float, he looked as excited as the people on the streets.

The confetti and the streams of toilet paper continued to fly through the air. People snapped

## JAY-Z AND THE YANKEES

In his song "Empire State of Mind," Jay-Z raps, "I made the Yankee hat more famous than a Yankee can."[3] Whether or not this is true, there's no doubt Jay-Z and the Yankees have been good for one another. A snippet of "Empire State of Mind" has played before Jeter's at bat. When Rodriguez stepped up to the plate, one of two Jay-Z songs ("Already Home" or "Reminder") blasted through the loudspeaker. And second baseman Robinson Cano chose the Jay-Z song "Run This Town" to introduce him as he took his turn in the batter's box.

The rapper is so popular in New York that he was asked to perform before game two of the 2009 World Series. Earlier that day, the Yankees organization let Jay-Z walk around the field. He said the experience made him feel like a kid again. While in the infield he pretended to throw a runner out at home. In the outfield he leaped against the wall as though he were robbing a batter of a home run.

His partnership with the Yankees didn't end after the 2009 World Series. The next year, the Yankees sold merchandise with his name on it, including a Yankees hat and jersey.

Jay-Z performed "Empire State of Mind" during the Yankees celebration.

pictures on their cameras and phones. Finally,
the parade reached its end at city hall. Michael
Bloomberg, the mayor of New York City,
congratulated the players and gave a speech. Then
he made a special announcement: the day's events
would be concluded with a song.

## AN "EMPIRE STATE OF MIND"

What was the song? "Empire State of Mind," of course. Released in October 2009, Jay-Z's hip-hop hit had already become the Yankees's unofficial anthem. The crowd roared as the bass thumped. Piano notes began just as Jay-Z stepped onto the stage.

"Yeah, I'm out that Brooklyn," Jay-Z rapped. "Now I'm down in Tribeca."[4] The song was greeted like a grand finale—the last, best part of a fireworks show. Players and fans alike shouted and swayed to the music.

What they may not have realized in their excitement was that Jay-Z's song was not only a New York sports anthem, but it was also telling the story of Jay-Z's rise from poverty to riches. By describing New York in a way that included the

## VOCALS ON "EMPIRE STATE OF MIND"

Earlier in 2009, Jay-Z performed "Empire State of Mind" at the MTV Music Awards. The song includes vocals and a chorus—often referred to as a "hook"—that is usually sung by soul singer Alicia Keys. When Keys isn't available, Bridget Kelly does the hook. Kelly shared the stage with Jay-Z after the World Series and while performing on the television show *Saturday Night Live*.

Jay-Z is a hip-hop icon.

city's glamour and grit, he was chronicling his own life in the city. Just as the lyrics state, Jay-Z grew up in a poor neighborhood in Brooklyn and eventually made it to Tribeca, one of the world's most fashionable neighborhoods. How had he traveled from some of the most dangerous places in New York to this very stage in front of city hall? How had a shy kid from the streets become one of the most successful rappers, business moguls, and cultural icons in the world?

||||||||||

Shawn grew up in inner city
New York.

CHAPTER 2

# Growing Up

|||||||||||||||||||||||||||||||||||||||||||||||||||||||||||||||||||||||||||||||||||

Jay-Z was born Shawn Corey Carter on December 4, 1969, in Brooklyn, New York. Shawn spent his childhood there along with his older siblings Eric, Michelle, and Andrea, parents Adnis Reeves and Gloria Carter, and some extended family.

The Carter family lived in the Marcy Houses projects, which was one of the poorest, roughest areas of the city. In Marcy, shards of glass covered grassy

Shawn grew up in the rugged Marcy Houses projects
in the Bedford-Stuyvesant neighborhood of Brooklyn.

areas where kids played. Dealers sold drugs on the
streets. Violence was always a possibility. When he
was nine years old, Shawn saw an older kid named
Benny shot and killed. Before he died, Benny had
often brought Shawn and other neighborhood kids
to baseball practice.

But as a kid, Shawn's sense of adventure took
the place of fear. Marcy was his world, and he
roamed it freely. He was four years old when he
rode a two-wheel bicycle for the first time. Because

of the bike's size, he had to position one foot through the top bar, a maneuver that made it look like he was facing sideways. To this day, Jay-Z can remember the amazed faces of Marcy residents as they watched such a young boy pedal around the neighborhood on a ten-speed bike. He can also remember an abandoned boat that was left on the side of the block. Shawn and his friends played in this boat as if it were a jungle gym.

## A CHILDHOOD WITH MUSIC

While growing up, Shawn heard and loved lots of styles of music. His parents had a huge music collection that included albums by Michael Jackson, Prince, and Marvin Gaye. Records were stacked floor-to-ceiling in the Carter household. The whole family listened and danced to music every Saturday as they cleaned the apartment.

## MUSIC AFTER BEDTIME

Shawn's parents often held music parties in the family apartment. The parties occurred at night, when Shawn was supposed to be in bed. Instead of sleeping, he would sneak into the front room in his pajamas and watch the adults dance.

When Shawn was in sixth grade, he could already read at a twelfth-grade level. In addition to his talent with words, Shawn has always had a photographic memory. This means when he sees something once he can remember it perfectly later. His verbal and memory skills have played a key role in becoming a successful rapper.

Shawn and his sister Andrea even made up choreographed dance routines together.

When he was nine years old, Shawn heard rap music for the first time. The music was different from the kind he listened to at home. Shawn was walking around in his neighborhood when he discovered a circle of teenagers laughing and clapping. They were all listening to another teen, a kid who stood in the middle of the circle and was rhyming about anything and everything—the clothes people were wearing, basketball, and whatever else came to his mind. He went on for a long time, whirling around and around and looking at everyone in the circle. The crowd couldn't get enough—and neither could Shawn.

Later that night, he jotted down rhymes of his own. The words poured out of him. When he had enough for a song, he gave himself a beat by slapping the table or his window. He started carrying a notebook everywhere he went. If a new lyric occurred to him, he stopped whatever else he was doing and wrote down the words.

## RAP'S GROWING POPULARITY

By the early 1980s, rap—which developed in the United States in the mid-1970s—was making its way into the realm of mainstream music. Hip-hop groups started appearing on popular television shows. (Although the terms have some distinctions, Jay-Z considers the terms hip-hop and rap to be synonymous.) The Funky Four Plus One More performed on *Saturday Night Live*; the Rock Steady Crew was featured on *ABC Nightly News*. Hip-hop may not have had the reach of rock and roll, but it was becoming a legitimate music choice on radio stations and late-night talk shows.

In the Marcy projects, rap had pretty much become the only musical choice by the early 1980s. Hip-hop songs blared from boom boxes, car radios, and out of the mouths of performers on the street. As a kid, Shawn and his sister choreographed and performed their own dance moves as they listened to their favorite hip-hop songs. As the years went by, artists such as Run-DMC began to rap more honestly about the tough neighborhoods they grew up in. Shawn felt, for the first time, that his own experiences were being captured in the songs he listened to.

In the 1980s, rap groups such as Run-DMC helped
increase the popularity of rap music.

When he wasn't writing or singing, he read the
dictionary to expand his vocabulary and lyrical
possibilities. Shawn was not yet Jay-Z. But he was
quickly becoming a rapper.

# THE LOSS OF A HERO

In 1980, when Shawn was 11 years old, his father, Adnis, left the family. The reason for his departure was revenge. Adnis's brother, Shawn's uncle, had been stabbed to death, and people in the community felt they knew who had committed the murder. When the police didn't do anything, Adnis vowed to track down the killer. He never accomplished this goal, but he never returned home either. The loss of his father was devastating to Shawn. He was at an age, he said, when his father seemed like a superhero.

Shawn had lost a mentor, and he sought out others to fulfill that role. Eventually, he found two men to guide him through his teen years. One of them was a rapper. The other was a drug dealer.

IIIIIIIIII

## RAP IS POETRY |||||||||||||||||||||||||||||||||||||||||||||||||||||||||||||||||

The rhymes Shawn first heard on the street were called couplets. A couplet is two consecutive lines that typically rhyme with one another. Couplets are often found in poems, but they're an important part of songs too. Jay-Z considers rap a form of poetry.

Jaz-O played a key role in Jay-Z's development as a rapper.

## CHAPTER 3

# The Road to Rap

||||||||||||||||||||||||||||||||||||||||||||||

**W**hen Shawn was 15, he met his first mentor, a local rapper named Jonathan "Jaz-O" Burks. Though Shawn— by this time known as Jay-Z—looked up to the 20-year-old Jaz-O, their first meeting wasn't designed to be friendly. The two were paired against each other to compete in a rap battle. In these battles, one rapper is pitted against another in a contest of skill. Verbal

Different theories exist about how Jay-Z's nickname came to be. Some say it's a tribute to the J and Z subway lines that come to a stop by his childhood neighborhood. Others claim he's paying tribute to his childhood friend and rap mentor, Jaz-O. Jay-Z denies both of these theories. He says the name is simply a shortened version of his childhood nickname, Jazzy.

sparring ensues. Improvised rhymes are spat back and forth. The goal is to never back down to the other's taunts and boasts, and this goal can bring out the best in both rappers.

When Jaz-O saw the scrawny teen he was supposed to compete against, Jaz-O called for a truce. Instead of rapping *against* each other, Jaz-O suggested the two of them rap *with* each other. That's when he realized how talented Jay-Z really was. Like everyone else who had witnessed Jay-Z rap, Jaz-O was wowed by the 15-year-old's lyrical abilities and decided to act as his mentor. Jay-Z clearly had talent, but he needed to learn technique too. Under Jaz-O's tutelage, Jay-Z learned the fundamentals of all poetry: "metaphor, simile, onomatopoeia," Jaz-O recalls, "things that most rap artists would say to you, 'What is that?'"[1]

Jaz-O also encouraged Jay-Z to practice as much as possible, and Jay-Z took this advice to heart. Jay-Z attended George Westinghouse High School. Other former Westinghouse students who became rappers include Busta Rhymes and the Notorious B.I.G. (also called Biggie Smalls). Though Jay-Z didn't know Biggie in high school, he remembers passing him in the school hallways. At high school, Jay-Z was often found standing on one end of the cafeteria, banging out beats on a lunch table and

## SHOOTING HIS BROTHER

Today, Jay-Z talks openly about his past career as a drug dealer, but he is not always willing to talk about the time he shot his older brother, Eric. Jay-Z was 12 years old and was furious at 16-year-old Eric for stealing a ring from him. The shot may have been meant as a warning—he may have intended to miss—but it hit his brother in the shoulder.

Eric was hospitalized but chose not to press charges. The fact that Jay-Z as a 12-year-old had a gun and that he never faced legal ramifications is evidence of how violent his neighborhood was at the time. Bullet wounds were common enough that they often didn't raise much alarm. Though Jay-Z is reluctant to discuss the incident in interviews, he rapped about it in the song "You Must Love Me." According to the song, Jay-Z shot the gun because his brother had "hurt [his] pride."[2] He also has said that he wanted Eric to talk him out of pulling the trigger.

improvising lyrics. But soon, his performances at school came to an end. Jay-Z decided to quit high school to sell drugs.

||||||||||||||||||||||||||||||||||||||||||||||||||||||

## DEALING DRUGS

The life of a drug dealer is often glamorized in hip-hop songs and their music videos. Dealers are shown driving expensive cars and surrounded by beautiful women. For many inner-city teenagers, these images influence their decisions to start dealing drugs. Jay-Z saw the fancy car, which he called "the trappings of drug dealing," and he couldn't resist the promise of driving one himself.[3]

But the glamorization is often not reality. A drug dealer typically has only two fates: prison or death. Jay-Z witnessed the dangers of drug dealing

## RAP'S METER AND FLOW ||||||||||||||||||||||||||||||||||||||||||||||||||

Rap involves two different types of rhythm: meter and flow. The meter is simply a song's beat. It is steady and constant like the second hand of a clock. The flow is produced by the rapper's voice and words. The flow can move within the beat or around it. It can speed up and slow down. Jay-Z compares the flow to the human heart, which also changes speed and tempo depending on the situation.

As a teenager, Jay-Z began selling drugs to make money.

firsthand while growing up. A man who supplied drugs for him was viciously killed when Jay-Z was young. Jay-Z later said,

> Thirteen-year-old kids don't wake up one day and say, "Okay, I just wanna sell drugs on my mother's stoop, hustle on my block till . . . [people] come look for me and start shooting out my mom's

*living room windows." Trust me, no one wakes up in the morning and wants to do that.*[4]

But this did not deter Jay-Z from selling drugs. Jay-Z's motivations for quitting school to become a drug dealer had a lot to do with money and food. Before Jay-Z started dealing drugs, his family was so poor that they couldn't always afford to eat. He often spent time at friends' houses because they had food in the fridge. Once Jay-Z started dealing, he used some of the money he earned to help his family eat.

Drug dealing, which is also referred to as hustling, offered the possibility of escape for Jay-Z. Unlike many of the other dealers he knew, he didn't sell drugs in his own neighborhood. When he was 18, he began taking the train to Trenton, New Jersey, to stay with his friend DeHaven Irby.

## STUDYING HIS MOVES

Jay-Z often played basketball with Irby on Brooklyn's outdoor courts. Today, Irby says Jay-Z was a good shooter but would "do a lot of studying before he'd make a move."[5] This tendency to study his moves was also apparent in Jay-Z's decision to sell drugs. He didn't start traveling to Trenton until Irby had already moved there and checked out the drug scene.

By his late teens, Jay-Z was living full time in Trenton, New Jersey, selling drugs.

Before moving to New Jersey, Irby had lived across the hall from Jay-Z, and the two remained close despite living in different states. After Irby moved away, he convinced Jay-Z to make the trips to Trenton. When Jay-Z arrived, the two began selling drugs on a dead-end street in the neighborhood. After a while, Jay-Z stopped taking the train back and forth and started living in New Jersey full time. His music career became an afterthought. But it wouldn't be for long.

‖‖‖‖‖‖‖

In 1988, Jay-Z's rap career got a leg up when Jaz-O invited Jay-Z on tour with him.

## CHAPTER 4

# More Rapping and Dealing

‖‖‖‖‖‖‖‖‖‖‖‖‖‖‖‖‖‖‖‖‖‖‖‖‖‖‖‖‖‖‖‖‖‖‖‖‖‖‖‖‖‖‖‖‖‖‖‖‖‖‖‖‖‖‖‖‖‖‖‖‖‖‖

I n 1988, when Jay-Z was 19 years old, he got a phone call from Jaz-O. The hip-hop mentor had good news: he had signed with EMI Records, a British record label, for almost $500,000. At the time, the amount seemed absurdly high. Back in the states, rappers were being paid much less, and some were not paid at all. Some had signed onto a label and received a car instead of cash. Jaz-O had hit the jackpot, but that wasn't all. He wanted to know if Jay-Z would tour with him in London, England. Jay-Z said yes.

Jay-Z had rarely left the East Coast, but for a few months he got to live in London's Notting Hill neighborhood. While in London, Jay-Z and Jaz-O showed up to Jaz-O's New Year's Eve album release party in a Cadillac limousine. Jay-Z also played Jaz-O's sidekick in music videos. At the time, Will Smith, whose stage name was the Fresh Prince, starred in some of the most popular hip-hop music videos. Smith's music videos feature him bobbing his head and grinning. Smith's hip-hop was a far cry from the hard-edged, reality-based hip-hop that Jaz-O and Jay-Z typically performed.

But the two buddies couldn't argue with Smith's success, and for a few songs, they tried to emulate his laid-back, fun style. In the song

## RAPPING DIFFERENTLY

Before becoming a movie star, Will Smith was the first person to win a Grammy Award in the Best Rap Performance category at the 1988 Grammys. He won for his song "Parents Just Don't Understand." He also starred in the hit 1990s sitcom *The Fresh Prince of Bel-Air*. His early success helped hip-hop join the mainstream, but his style of music didn't represent the street culture that Jay-Z and other rappers sought to explore.

Rapper Will Smith's easygoing style contrasted with the edgier styles of Jaz-O and Jay-Z.

"Hawaiian Sophie," they traded in their street clothes for Hawaiian shirts. In the 1989 video for "The Originators," Jay-Z wore a shirt with red and white stripes. Compared to the songs Jay-Z would perform later in his career, the music the duo made in London was light and fluffy. Despite his significant contract, Jaz-O's album was barely promoted by EMI, and he never experienced lasting stardom.

But those who were aware of the album couldn't help noticing Jay-Z's talent, even though it was buried under layers of silliness. His small but impressive vocal appearances in Jaz-O's songs created his reputation as a rapper to watch. When Jay-Z got back from his London trip, rapper Big Daddy Kane offered Jay-Z a spot on his bus tour in 1989. Kane was one of the top rappers of the era, and Jay-Z wasn't the only talented artist on the bus. Hip-hop artists MC Serch, Queen Latifah, and Tupac Shakur—considered one of the all-time

## FEAR OF FAILURE

Jay-Z was crushed when Jaz-O didn't make it big, but it took Jay-Z a while to understand the severity of his disappointment. A few years later, during a conversation with his girlfriend, the weight of what had happened in London really hit him. He finally realized his fear of failing in the same way Jaz-O had was holding Jay-Z back in his music career and life.

Jay-Z impressed audiences when he had the opportunity to rap on Big Daddy Kane's tour.

greats—were included in the tour. And Jay-Z wasn't just there to tag along between concerts. When Kane took breaks during performances,

Jay-Z was sometimes given the opportunity to freestyle rap in front of huge, enthusiastic crowds.

In addition to asking Jay-Z to tour with him, Kane also put Jay-Z in one of his music videos. The song "Show and Prove" features several famous rappers, including Scoob Lover, Sauce Money, and Shyheim, who was 16 at the time. In the video, each rapper takes a turn showcasing his individual rapping style while standing surrounded by a group of listeners. The rap circle must have looked something like the one Jay-Z discovered as a kid. The difference was that now he had a chance to be the performer inside the circle.

## DRUG LIFE

These music videos and shows may have offered Jay-Z the excitement of being a real rapper, but

## LEARNING SHOWMANSHIP

Big Daddy Kane was a terrific showman. He had dancers on stage and wore suits without undershirts. Sometimes he would start a popular song and then interrupt himself midlyric with another song. Jay-Z credits Kane for teaching him a lot about putting together a great live show.

Part of Jay-Z's talent is his remarkable ability to memorize songs without ever having to write them down. One time, during a recording session featuring Jay-Z and rapper Sauce Money, the song's producer became irritated by what he perceived to be Jay-Z's lack of preparation. Jay-Z had been in the studio for several hours, and he had spent most of the time joking with Sauce. As far as the producer could tell, Jay-Z hadn't even come up with any lyrics to rap. After being scolded for wasting time and money, Jay-Z turned his attention to the track of music that was playing. He spent a few moments mumbling and scribbling in his notebook. He appeared to study what he'd just written and then made his way into the sound booth.

As Jay-Z recorded his lyrics, the producer opened Jay-Z's notebook. The pages were blank. He'd merely pretended to write down the words he was currently belting out in the sound booth.

what they didn't offer was money. Besides being given food and a place to sleep, his time on Big Daddy Kane's bus was entirely unpaid. When the tour was over, Jay-Z went back to dealing drugs to earn his living.

By this time, Jay-Z was in his 20s, and he and Irby had expanded their business to other states. They divided their time between New York, New

As a drug dealer, Jay-Z was beginning to be aware of the damage he was doing to individuals and his community. As a teen, he had been able to ignore the effects of drug addiction on his customers. Sometimes he even laughed at them.

But in his twenties, he started to feel a lingering sense of remorse that only got worse the longer he continued hustling. He didn't fully recognize the gravity of this remorse until after he'd quit the work entirely.

Jersey, Maryland, and Virginia. The reason for all the travel was supply and demand. In New York and New Jersey, the high number of drug dealers drove down the price of drugs. The number of dealers in Maryland and Virginia was smaller, so Jay-Z and Irby could charge more for the drugs they sold. Later, Jay-Z showed the same business sense in the music world, but during this time, rap took a backseat to selling drugs.

Though he was only in his early twenties and had put hip-hop on hold for a while, Jay-Z had still managed to work alongside people in the music business who believed he had what it took to become a successful hip-hop artist. Jay-Z believed pursuing that path was worth a shot. And

Jay-Z decided to pursue a rap career when he was in his twenties.

after years of hustling, he had important stories to communicate through his music.

||||||||||

Jay-Z got serious about his rapping in the mid-1990s.

CHAPTER 5

# Convincing the Reasonable Doubters

|||||||||||||||||||||||||||||||||||||||||||||||||

It was DJ Clark Kent who finally convinced Jay-Z he could become a successful rapper. Kent was a talent scout for Atlantic Records and had been telling Jay-Z to rap full time for years. Finally, in the mid-1990s, Jay-Z heeded his advice and recorded most of the songs that would become his first album, *Reasonable Doubt*. Recording his own music took not only courage but also lots of money. The producer and the sound engineer needed to get paid. Along with these specialists' fees, there was also a charge for studio time. In the 1990s, a four-hour time slot could cost as much as $10,000. Jay-Z paid for this amount with the money he'd made selling drugs.

DJ Kent hoped Jay-Z's financial commitment would result in a deal with a major record label. But it turned out none of the major labels were interested in Jay-Z's songs—not even Atlantic Records, despite Kent's best efforts at convincing them to sign the rapper. The reasons Jay-Z went unsigned are not fully known. Some speculate that the executives simply didn't understand the music. Jay-Z's songs were loaded with poetic strategies such as metaphors and similes. Others say the music was too hard-edged for the executives. The purpose of Jay-Z's rap was to reflect what was

## RAP ROLES

Most rap songs involve both a DJ and an MC. A DJ, or disk jockey, provides the mix of music that is the backdrop for a hip-hop song. An MC, or mic controller, provides the lyrics to the song. As an MC, Jay-Z is usually quick to praise the work of the DJs he collaborates with.

DJ Clark Kent persuaded Jay-Z to pursue a solo career.

actually going on in the streets where he grew up, and according to entertainment lawyer Donald David, record labels were "scared of the violence" in Jay-Z's lyrics.[1]

## MARKETING WITH DASH

Whatever the reason, the labels were not interested in *Reasonable Doubt*, and at that point Jay-Z had to choose whether he was going to give up or find another way to sell the album. He opted to sell the album without a record label. Kent introduced Jay-Z to the up-and-coming businessman Damon Dash—a man who was full of ideas and ambition. The first time Jay-Z met him, Dash did almost all the talking. This was not out of the ordinary. Despite all the boasting Jay-Z does in his songs, he's typically shy when meeting people for the first time. At that first meeting, Dash shared a whirlwind of ideas for how to sell Jay-Z's album, and Jay-Z found the man's confidence reassuring.

Together, the two of them began marketing Jay-Z's album out of the backs of their cars. They

## DYNAMIC DUO

Even before Damon Dash partnered with Jay-Z, his efforts to promote the people he represented were bold and creative. When he hosted music events, he gave out free bottles of champagne to the first 100 women in line. DJ Kent thought Dash's big promotional ideas would match Jay-Z's big-time talent perfectly.

Damon Dash worked with Jay-Z to promote Jay-Z's
first album on the streets of New York.

traveled around New York City, blasting his music
from their cars' speakers and hawking his album
like street vendors. They distributed *Reasonable
Doubt* flyers, stickers, and shirts throughout the

Many rappers are accused of promoting violence in their songs. Jay-Z's defense of his rap is that violent songs don't necessarily promote violent behavior. Instead, they reflect and explore the violence already happening in poor, urban communities. This violence often follows rappers even after they've achieved fame and fortune. Notorious B.I.G. and Tupac Shakur are famous examples of rappers who were killed despite having "escaped" the streets. Jay-Z commented,

"The world wants to think [that] people are drawn to violence [in songs] but when you live in the ghetto you see violence all the time, so that's not the real excitement. If they want to see violence, all they have to do is go home."[2]

Jay-Z's goal isn't to encourage violence but to tell the story of his life and his neighborhood. By doing so, he can give attention to a community often overlooked. Of course, Jay-Z isn't the only one with this goal. He credits hip-hop as a whole for giving an entire generation of ghetto kids a voice in popular culture.

city. The duo took their merchandise and Jay-Z's talent anywhere and everywhere, from clubs to barbershops, and all of their hard work eventually paid off. *Reasonable Doubt* became one of the most popular albums in the city, and record labels started to take notice.

Two labels, Freeze Records and Priority Records, joined forces to sell *Reasonable Doubt* across the country on June 25, 1996. Within a year, the album sold 420,000 copies, and that didn't include all the records Jay-Z and Dash had already peddled in New York. In addition to its popularity with fans, music critics loved the album. The songs may have been gritty, but they were also undeniably artistic. Jay-Z combined smooth soul music with lyrical but unflinching stories about dealing drugs, and the contrast created what is now considered a classic hip-hop album.

||||||||||||||||||||||||||||||||||||||||||||||||||||||||||

## ROC-A-FELLA RECORDS

Jay- Z's album had become a hit, but when he went to Freeze Records and Priority Records and asked for the money he'd earned, he was turned away empty-handed. He was told the money wasn't there yet and he'd have to wait. The situation struck Jay-Z as unfair, and he decided to leave the labels and take his record with him.

He was able to do this for two reasons. First, he and Dash had made sure to keep the rights to Jay-Z's album when they signed their one-year contract, a move that most young musicians don't think to make. Second, the two of them—along with a third partner, Kareem "Biggs" Burke—had created a company of their own called Roc-A-Fella Records in 1995.

For now, Roc-A-Fella was used as a way to sell Jay-Z's music. Through the company, Jay-Z and Dash orchestrated a bidding war to decide which record company would gain the rights to rerelease *Reasonable Doubt*. Def Jam Records was interested in the rerelease rights to the album, but to acquire these rights, Def Jam had to buy a partial stake in

## NAMING AN EMPIRE ||||||||||||||||||||||||||||||||||||||||||||||||||||||||||||||||||||||||||||

Roc-A-Fella Records was named after turn-of-the-century billionaire John D. Rockefeller. Like the Rockefeller name, Jay-Z and Damon Dash wanted their company to signify wealth and success.

Jay-Z launched Roc-A-Fella Records and would be linked to it throughout his career, even after becoming famous.

Roc-A-Fella as well. Because it was only a 33 percent stake, rather than the usual 50 percent, Roc-A-Fella would still earn the bulk of any album's profits. This meant that Jay-Z's music would be sold as a Def Jam product, but Roc-A-Fella would be the label making more money from the product.

||||||||||

By the late 1990s, Jay-Z's rap career was going strong. He had released three albums by 1999.

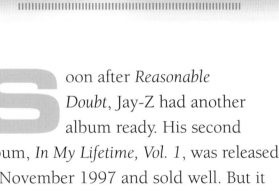

## CHAPTER 6
# More Music

||||||||||||||||||||||||||||||||||||||||||||||||||||||||||||||||||||||||||||||||

**S**oon after *Reasonable Doubt*, Jay-Z had another album ready. His second album, *In My Lifetime, Vol. 1*, was released in November 1997 and sold well. But it didn't compare to the success of his third album, *Vol. 2 . . . Hard Knock Life*, which was released in November 1998. In the United States alone, *Hard Knock Life* sold more than 5 million copies.

The album eventually won the 1998 Grammy for Best Rap Album, but Jay-Z

Jay-Z wasn't the first rapper to boycott the Grammys. Ever since the 1988 Grammys, when rap was given its own award categories but no airtime, hip-hop artists and the Grammys have had a rocky relationship. That year, Will Smith, DJ Jazzy Jeff, and LL Cool J decided to skip the award ceremony.

wasn't at the award show to receive it. The year of the ceremony, 1999, the Recording Academy, the organization behind the Grammys, decided not to televise the portions where rap awards were given out. As a result, Jay-Z and many other rappers decided to boycott the event. Officially, the Recording Academy claimed they meant no disrespect; they simply didn't have enough time to fit the rap awards into the televised portion of the ceremony. Still, Jay-Z felt hip-hop was not being given the recognition it deserved. Years later, he described the snub in terms of dinner guests. It was "like people invite you over to their house for dinner," he said, "and then tell you you have to eat in the basement."[1]

|||||||||||||||||||||||||||||||||||||||||||||||||||||||

## CRITICISM

While Jay-Z was being critical of the Grammys, some hard-core hip-hop fans were being critical of him. Some critics and serious rap fans thought Jay-Z had sold out on his last couple albums. In its review of *In My Lifetime*, *Rolling Stone* magazine wrote that Jay-Z was in search of "a larger pop prize, to the detriment of his art."[2] In a lot of ways, Jay-Z agreed with his critics. He didn't deny that he had made a conscious decision to slow down and slick up his songs. His patented rapid-fire delivery and some of the grit of his first album's lyrics were missing from the album. Jay-Z fully acknowledged these changes, but he made no apology for them. Simply put, he was out to sell records and gain a wider audience, and in *Hard Knock Life* he did

## "HARD KNOCK LIFE"

The title track from *Hard Knock Life* is one of the album's best-known songs. In the song, Jay-Z's hard-hitting, autobiographical lyrics contrast and blend with the "Hard Knock Life" melody from the musical *Annie*. The story of a red-headed orphan girl might seem like it has nothing to do with an inner-city, African-American boy, but Jay-Z points out that many kids living on the streets are fatherless and feel like orphans.

both. *Rolling Stone* magazine would later name *Hard Knock Life* one of the best albums of the 1990s. The magazine would praise the way Jay-Z made "every track his own with massive boasts, state-of-the-art flows, [and] vivid underworld portraits drawn in only a handful of words."[3]

## BUILDING A BRAND

As he gained a wider audience, Jay-Z performed more frequently. While on stage, Jay-Z often wore clothing made by Iceberg. As he looked out at his audience, he realized that many of them sported Iceberg apparel too. He believed this to be more than a coincidence. Jay-Z and Dash scheduled a meeting with Iceberg and pointed out that Jay-Z had been marketing the company's clothing for free. The duo said they would be happy to continue promoting Iceberg, but the apparel company should compensate them for doing so.

When Iceberg declined their offer, Jay-Z and Dash decided to start their own clothing line in 1999. Playing off the Roc-A-Fella name, the pair began Rocawear, a clothing brand that would eventually become a multimillion-dollar success.

Rapper Trey Songz promoted Rocawear in 2010 and 2011. The style of clothing represented the urban style Jay-Z wore.

Before it took off, though, it was nothing more than a few sewing machines in their office. The original plan was to make all the clothing themselves—an idea that was quickly exposed as naive. For one thing, neither they nor anyone they knew was very good at sewing. Each individual T-shirt took them three weeks to complete.

The duo needed help with their business plan for Rocawear, and they got it from Russell Simmons, the founder of both Def Jam Records and Phat Farm clothing. Simmons referred them to people who had experience in the clothing industry. Soon Rocawear was producing not only T-shirts but also jeans, sweatshirts, sneakers, and even cologne. With Rocawear, Jay-Z and his partners captured the style of the streets. The clothes were baggy and featured lots of pockets. In its first 18 months, the Rocawear brand made $80 million in revenue.

And Roc-A-Fella wasn't done. Jay-Z and Dash made a deal to endorse a brand of Vodka, Armadale, and a brand of champagne, Armand de Brignac. The pair branched out in the music world too. Rather than just promote Jay-Z, they

## HELPING A YOUNGER RAPPER

Today, Memphis Bleek is a famous rapper in his own right, but it was Jay-Z who discovered him. The first time Jay-Z recruited him to perform on an album, Bleek was a skinny, hungry kid. When Jay-Z offered to pay for his food after stopping at a fast-food restaurant, Bleek ordered six cheeseburgers and ate every one of them. But he was also hungry for fame and success. Bleek's first solo album, *Coming of Age*, was released in August 1999. Jay-Z contributed vocals to the song "What You Think of That."

Jay-Z helped Bleek get his start. He performed with the new rapper and even added vocals to a song on Bleek's album.

began representing other rappers, including Beanie Sigel, Freeway, and Memphis Bleek. Jay-Z made lyrical appearances on each rapper's first album, guaranteeing the album would be a success.

||||||||||

Jay-Z was irate when his fourth album was leaked before its release date.

# Crime and Relationships

||||||||||||||||||||||||||||||||||||||||||||||||||||||||||||||||||||||||||||||||||||||

I n 1999, Jay-Z was getting ready to release his fourth album, *Volume 3 . . . Life and Times of S. Carter.* About a month before the official release date, he got word the album was being bootlegged on the streets. Today, musicians lose millions of dollars due to file sharing and the illegal downloading of their music, and bootlegging is little more than an afterthought. But in 1999, the primary way to steal and make a profit off of someone's album was to sell it on the streets before its official release date.

Jay-Z was furious when he found out. He interrogated everyone who had helped make the album, and they all blamed record executive Lance Rivera. When Jay-Z spotted Rivera at a nightclub, a fight broke out. According to Jay-Z, he was so angry with Rivera that he blacked out. Later, what he remembered was the chaos of the brawl as his friends fought Rivera's. In the incident, Jay-Z stabbed Rivera in the stomach with a five-inch (13-cm) blade.

By the time Jay-Z turned himself in to the police the next day, the press was all over the story. At first, Jay-Z claimed he was innocent but eventually admitted he had stabbed Rivera and settled the case out of court. Jay-Z was able to avoid spending time in prison by paying Rivera somewhere between $500,000 and $1 million. Jay-Z was also given three years of probation. He said the ordeal taught him a lot about self-control. "I had a choice," he said. "There was no reason to put my life on the line, and the lives of everyone

Jay-Z was arrested for assaulting Rivera in 1999.

who depends on me, because of a momentary loss of control."[1]

After they filmed a music video together, rumors began circulating in the media that Beyoncé and Jay-Z were dating.

## JAY-Z AND BEYONCÉ

Jay-Z was still on probation when he asked singer Beyoncé Knowles to contribute to one of his songs and be in its music video with him. Beyoncé was the most famous member of the group Destiny's Child, and she was just beginning to launch her solo career. When Jay-Z needed a female singer, Beyoncé immediately came to mind.

The pair recorded the song "03 Bonnie and Clyde" in 2002, and the music video features the two of them as both robbers and lovers. Throughout the video, the authorities pursue them and in every case, Jay-Z and Beyoncé evade capture. In several scenes Jay-Z has his arm draped around Beyoncé's shoulder.

The video helped fuel rampant speculation. Was the rap industry's king in a relationship with the up-and-coming pop diva? The two made an

## IMAGE VERSUS REALITY

One of the reasons many people found Jay-Z's relationship with Beyoncé confusing had to do with Jay-Z's lyrics regarding women. In songs such as 2001's "Girls, Girls, Girls," Jay-Z appears to brag about the number of women he has been involved with. In 1999's "Big Pimpin'," he declares, "I'll be forever mackin'."[2]

But appearances can be deceiving. Chenise Wilson, a close friend of Jay-Z's, reported that Jay-Z was never the ladies' man he claims to be in his songs. Also, the narrative voice in a Jay-Z song might not be his own. Instead, it could come from an invented persona. Many hip-hop artists use a persona as a means of writing shocking and extreme lyrics. For example, rapper Eminem's persona, Slim Shady, is in many ways the rapper's alter ego. Lastly, Jay-Z's raps could have been misunderstood on a lyrical level. His raps have used terms that are often derogatory toward women. But Jay-Z says he doesn't use them in derogatory ways.

Jay-Z and Beyoncé performed "Crazy in Love" at the MTV Video Music Awards in 2003.

intriguing pair: Beyoncé was 20 years old and had cultivated a wholesome reputation; Jay-Z was 32 years old and had spent more than a decade rapping explicitly about the realities of life on the streets. The media continued to focus on the pair, and their relationship was confirmed in 2002. Soon after, news stories inaccurately reported the couple had broken up. The *Miami Herald* mused, "It sounds as though the music has stopped playing for Jay-Z and Beyoncé Knowles."[3]

But the music hadn't stopped. In the summer of 2003, Jay-Z showed up in Beyoncé's music video "Crazy in Love," a song that seemed to express the couple's actual feelings toward one another.

||||||||||||||||||||||||||||||||||||||||||||||||||||||||||

## A MISSING FATHER RETURNS

Along with romance, 2003 included another life-altering experience when Jay-Z reconciled with his father. At first, Jay-Z did not want to see the man who had abandoned him when he was a child, but Jay-Z's mother insisted on the reunion.

### CHART-TOPPING DUO ||||||||||||||||||||||||||||||||||||||||||||||||

Jay-Z and Beyoncé have been a chart-topping team. *Rolling Stone* magazine named Beyoncé's song "Crazy in Love" the third-best song of the first decade of the twenty-first century. Jay-Z's song "99 Problems" was just ahead of it in second place.

When Adnis didn't show up at the appointed time and place, Jay-Z was even more certain that he never needed to see the man again. His mother rescheduled the meeting anyway, and this time Adnis did show up. He and Jay-Z had a long, tough, one-sided conversation. Jay-Z pummeled his father with accusations and questions, and Adnis eventually apologized. To Jay-Z's surprise, he forgave his father instantly.

The quickness of his forgiveness may have had to do with his father's sickness. As a lifelong alcoholic, Adnis's liver was deteriorating. He died soon after reconnecting with Jay-Z but was able

## REASONS TO BE GRATEFUL

Before abandoning Jay-Z when he was nine years old, Adnis helped inspire Jay-Z's love of music. He also trained Jay-Z to pay attention to the details of his neighborhood. On several occasions he took Jay-Z to a restaurant, bought him french fries, and challenged him to look out the window and notice the smallest details possible. The dress a woman was wearing, the gestures two people made as they talked, the location of different stores—these were the sort of observations he expected his son to make. Jay-Z put his learned powers of observation to good use as a rapper.

When Jay-Z was a kid, he didn't know the real reason why his father left. His parents argued a lot, and he assumed these arguments explained his dad's departure. As an adult, Jay-Z finally learned about his uncle's murder. It was his father's need to avenge his brother's death that drove him out of the house and contributed to his alcohol abuse. While this desire for revenge didn't excuse his father's behavior, it at least gave it some context that Jay-Z could understand.

to spend the last few months of his life in an apartment purchased for him by his famous son.

Being able to forgive his father was an important event in Jay-Z's life. It allowed him to trust other people and let people into his life more freely—including his girlfriend, Beyoncé. By reconnecting with his father, Jay-Z ended one chapter in his life and started another.

|||||||||||

Jay-Z's concert at Madison Square Garden on November 25 was his final show before his 2003 retirement.

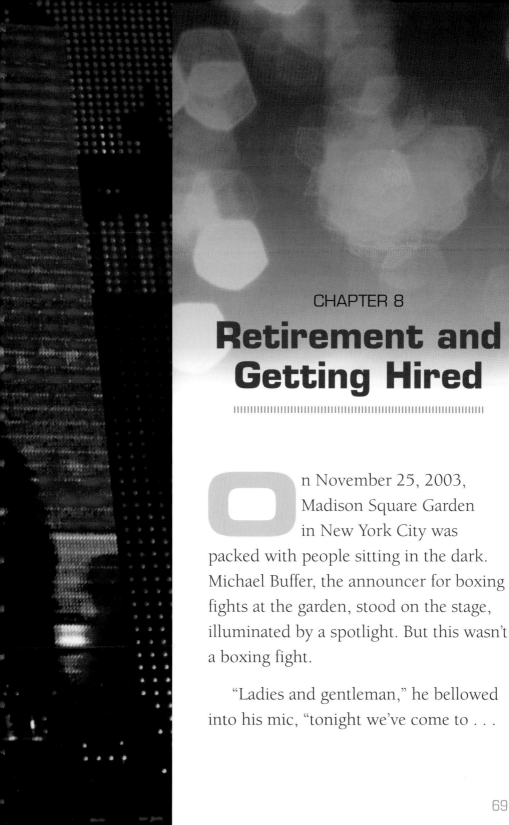

## CHAPTER 8

# Retirement and Getting Hired

||||||||||||||||||||||||||||||||||||||||||||||||||||||||||||||||||||||||||||||||||||||||||||

On November 25, 2003, Madison Square Garden in New York City was packed with people sitting in the dark. Michael Buffer, the announcer for boxing fights at the garden, stood on the stage, illuminated by a spotlight. But this wasn't a boxing fight.

"Ladies and gentleman," he bellowed into his mic, "tonight we've come to . . .

see and hear a legendary superstar. From Marcy projects, Bed-Stuy, Brooklyn, New York," Buffer continued, "presenting the one, the only, the undisputed, undefeated heavyweight champion of the world of hip-hop, he is . . . JAY-Z!"[1]

The lights came on and Jay-Z appeared. The crowd roared and rhymed along with the rapper. Soon, other celebrities joined him on stage, including Mary J. Blige, Beyoncé, Ghostface Killah, and Foxy Brown.

This concert was special because it was Jay-Z's final concert. Earlier that year, Jay-Z had announced his plan to retire from rapping. After the concert at the garden, Jay-Z would no longer perform live. His reasons for retiring were varied and complex, but they included a lack of motivation as a rapper—he'd achieved everything there was to achieve in that area— and his increased motivation as a businessman. Retirement would give him a chance to focus on his other talents in sales and marketing. It would also afford him the opportunity to develop and promote young rappers who were still trying to break into the industry. Besides, on November 14 he had released *The Black Album*. This was his

Jay-Z's jersey was lifted to the ceiling at Madison Square Garden.

eighth album in eight years, and Jay-Z was ready for a break.

That night, the concert ended with a giant New York Knicks basketball jersey with Jay-Z's name on it making its way to the garden's rafters. When an athlete's jersey is raised to the roof, the number on the jersey is considered permanently retired, which means no one on the athlete's former team will be allowed to wear a jersey with that number. By raising his own jersey to the rafters, Jay-Z was symbolically announcing his retirement from hip-hop.

When Jay-Z's basketball jersey was raised to the rafters of Madison Square Garden, it joined jerseys worn by the greatest players in Knicks basketball history. The numbers of Walt Frazier (10), Earl Monroe (15), and Patrick Ewing (33) have all been retired along with a handful of other Knicks greats. By retiring his own jersey, if only for the duration of the concert, Jay-Z was claiming a place for himself among Madison Square Garden's most-loved legends.

## FROM RAP SENSATION TO CEO

Jay-Z was involved in several ventures after his retirement from rapping, but the next big step he took in business happened in 2005, when Def Jam Records hired him to be the company's new chief executive officer (CEO). Since the 1980s, Def Jam had earned its reputation as the most prestigious record label in hip-hop. As a rapper, Jay-Z had been with the label since the rerelease of his first album, *Reasonable Doubt*, and his success had helped the company acquire this solid reputation. Now, as the president and CEO of the company, Jay-Z would have a chance to secure Def Jam's legacy and propel the label into the future.

It wouldn't be easy, though. Despite Def Jam's history of success, it had lost a lot of its most popular acts. And it wasn't just the amount of musical talent that Jay-Z found underwhelming; many of the Def Jam staff seemed to have lost their creative energy.

To boost this energy, Jay-Z took his employees on a two-day retreat. They stayed at the Tribeca Grand Hotel in Manhattan, and Jay-Z showed them old footage of Def Jam's first-ever sales pitch in 1984. He wanted his employees to observe the passion the label once had for finding and distributing its musical talent. He asked them to think back to the reasons they got into the music business in the first place.

Once back from the retreat, Jay-Z went to work finding and developing talent. His first huge hire was Rihanna, a 17-year-old Barbadian singer with a distinctive voice. Other performers he had success with include Young Jeezy, Ne-Yo, and even pop diva Mariah Carey.

According to several artists, what Jay-Z was particularly good at was helping them find their voices. When he signed hip-hop group The Roots,

Jay-Z has performed several times with Rihanna, who he signed while CEO of Def Jam Records.

many people were worried that he'd push them to tone down their edgy style in the hopes of selling more records, but the opposite was true. "Don't try to give me a hot radio single," he told Questlove, the group's drummer. "That's not who you are. Worry about making a great album, from the first cut to the last, a great Roots album."[2]

Jay-Z wanted his musicians to make songs that could be considered art, and to do so they needed to have the freedom to sing, compose, and perform in whatever ways served their styles best. Because he was a celebrated musician in his own right, Jay-Z had connections with people who could help Def Jam's musicians piece together the best possible albums. The day before The Roots's new album *Game Theory* was supposed to be completed, they were informed that the band Radiohead was going to charge them $700,000 to use a sample of their music. The sample was an important piece in one of The Roots's songs, so Questlove called Jay-Z

## NIGHTCLUB OWNER

In 2003, Jay-Z opened the 40/40 nightclub in New York City. He intended to begin a chain of nightclubs starting in New York; Atlantic City, New Jersey; and Las Vegas, Nevada and branching out to other places including Chicago, Illinois, and London. The Las Vegas location was sold in 2008, but in 2011 the 40/40 Web site promised a new club in London and in "select airports across the United States."[3]

Of all the big signings Jay-Z made as CEO of Def Jam, perhaps the most important to him personally was rapper Nas. For years, the two musicians had been rap rivals and even enemies. They had slung increasingly ugly insults back and forth in their songs and at their concerts. Jay-Z once said something so cruel that his mother demanded he apologize to Nas's family.

This war of words wasn't new to hip-hop. In the mid-1990s, rap's biggest names, Biggie and Tupac, were also archrivals. The words they spat at each other had so much venom that after both had been murdered, many people claimed their deaths were related.

Jay-Z and Nas were likely trying to create the same negative energy as Biggie and Tupac to increase their own sales numbers. Whatever the motives were for the feud, at some point Jay-Z grew tired of it. He threw a concert called "I Declare War" in 2005, but he declared just the opposite. On a stage made to look like the Oval Office, he introduced Nas, and together they called a truce by singing a song that included both of their lyrics. Shortly after, Nas signed with Def Jam Records.

and asked for his help. Jay-Z told him he'd see what he could do. A little while later, Thom Yorke, Radiohead's lead singer, called Questlove and said he could use the sample for free. Jay-Z was the one who made this conversation possible.

||||||||||

Nas, *above*, and Jay-Z reconciled
at Jay-Z's concert in 2005.

Jay-Z and his mother attended a fund-raiser for the Shawn Carter Scholarship Foundation, started by Jay-Z in 2003 to help underprivileged kids.

CHAPTER 9

# Giving Back

|||||||||||||||||||||||||||||||||||||||||||||||||||||||||||||||||

**B**y the mid-2000s, Jay-Z was one of the wealthiest musicians on the planet. By all accounts, he was living the high life. He owned two multimillion-dollar apartments in New York, luxury sports cars, and even part of an NBA team. But Jay-Z didn't use his money only to buy things for himself. He also donated money to several worthy causes.

||||||||||||||||||||||||||||||

## FUNDING EDUCATION

In 2003, Jay-Z founded the Shawn Carter Scholarship Foundation. The goal of the foundation is to help underprivileged kids attend college. From 2003 to 2005, the foundation handed out 50 college scholarships to 50 students from 50 different states. More than 750 students have received scholarships from the foundation. Though Jay-Z was a high school dropout, he doesn't encourage others to follow in his path. As he points out, there are very few successful rappers. On the other hand, there are many jobs available to those with college degrees.

## KEEPING A PROMISE TO HIMSELF

When Jay-Z was a kid, very few people escaped the poverty and day-to-day violence of his neighborhood. Those who did make it out of the Marcy projects often never returned. "They never came back to share the wisdom of how they made it," Jay-Z told Oprah in October 2009.[1] Consequently, Jay-Z promised himself that if he ever became successful, he would "come back here, grab somebody, and show him how it can be done."[2] Through the Shawn Carter Foundation and other philanthropic work, Jay-Z has helped at-risk youth transcend difficult childhoods.

Jay-Z also suffered personal tragedy in 2005. That summer, Jay-Z's nephew, Colleek Luckie, was killed in a car accident. He had been sitting shotgun in the Chrysler Jay-Z had given him as a graduation gift. Jay-Z couldn't help feeling partially responsible because he had bought the vehicle. Jay-Z and Luckie had been so close that Jay-Z thought of him almost as a son.

## NATIONAL SETBACK

On August 29, 2005, Hurricane Katrina ripped through Louisiana, leaving the city of New Orleans in ruins. Jay-Z found himself glued to the television as one horrific image after another revealed the devastation that had occurred. Beyond his grief, Jay-Z felt angry. The images he saw were not just of wreckage. He saw images of people who were in desperate situations and even facing death. In many cases, these people pleaded for help as helicopters dove in for pictures and then flew away. To this day, Jay-Z remembers seeing old women in wheelchairs who appeared to be dying right outside the New Orleans Superdome, where refugees had gathered. "Why isn't anyone doing anything?" he later remembered thinking.[3]

S.O.S.
Saving OurSelves
The BET☆ Relief Telethon

| Sean Combs & Shawn Carter | | 100 |
|---|---|---|
| | | DATE *September 9, 2005* |

PAY TO THE ORDER OF *The American Red Cross* $ *1,000,000*.00

*One Million Dollars* 00/00 —————————————————— DOLLARS

MEMO *Hurricane Katrina Relief*     *Sean Combs    Shawn Carter*

⑆000110203⑆ 71021 48265⑈ 2284

In 2005, Jay-Z and Sean "P. Diddy" Combs donated $1 million to the Red Cross for Hurricane Katrina relief.

Much of Jay-Z's anger and dismay were directed at the federal government, which he felt wasn't doing enough to help. The desperation he experienced helped fuel his compassion for the victims in New Orleans. Together with rapper Sean "P. Diddy" Combs, Jay-Z donated $1 million to the Red Cross. It was an immense act of charity, and yet even as Jay-Z gave the money, he still felt a little helpless. His distrust of the government was so severe, he had no faith in the Red Cross either. He was frustrated by his inability to track the money and make sure it made its way to those who really needed it.

|||||||||||||||||||||||||||||||||||||||||||||||||||||||||||||||||||||

## DOCUMENTING A GLOBAL ISSUE

In 2006, Jay-Z's frustration again led him to take action. He wanted to help people in need, and he wanted to see the proof of his help. In 2006, he partnered with the United Nations on a documentary called *Water for Life*. To film the documentary, he traveled to Africa and spent time with communities that had almost no water for drinking, bathing, or cooking. He was informed that more than 1 billion people in the world lack clean drinking water.

By spending time with families in water-scarce areas, Jay-Z learned firsthand about the difficulties some people have finding and retrieving enough water to survive. Along with others, he walked for long distances and across dangerous terrain to fill single buckets with water from a stream. Often, the

Jay-Z became a co-owner of the New Jersey Nets in 2004 when businessman Bruce Ratner's bid to buy the team was accepted. According to Ratner's proposal, the Nets would move out of New Jersey and into Brooklyn. This possibility sounded very appealing to Brooklyn-born Jay-Z, who decided to invest in the team. He and Beyoncé quickly became courtside regulars at Nets games.

The original plan was for the team to make the move to Brooklyn by 2008, but it became apparent that this wouldn't be possible. A group called Develop— Don't Destroy Brooklyn filed lawsuits to stop the new arena from being built. Plus, because of the economic recession, construction costs doubled. Ratner, the man who had masterminded the purchase of the Nets franchise, no longer had the money to move the team elsewhere.

In 2009, Mikhail Prokhorov, a Russian billionaire, bought Ratner's ownership of the team and announced that he still wanted to bring the team to Brooklyn. Construction of the stadium—the Barclays Center—was set to be completed in 2012. On September 26, 2011, Jay-Z announced that the New Jersey Nets, whom he still partly owns, will be renamed the Brooklyn Nets when they move to their new arena.

water wasn't sanitary. Bacteria in the water could cause rampant illness and even death.

On the trip, Jay-Z saw how drastically plumbing could improve an entire community's

Jay-Z and Beyoncé regularly attended Nets games after Jay-Z became co-owner of the team.

way of life. In one school he visited, the United Nations Children's Fund (UNICEF) donated a toilet, and the results were tremendous. Attendance at the school rose because the spread of germs and disease decreased. By filming the documentary, Jay-Z wanted to spread the word about water scarcity in Africa and to make a difference there.

||||||||||

Jay-Z's retirement was short lived.
In 2006, he returned to rapping,
and in 2008, he performed at the
Glastonbury Festival in England.

## CHAPTER 10

# Looking toward the Future

IIIIIIIIIIIIIIIIIIIIIIIIIIIIIIIIIIIIIIIIIIIIIIIIIIIIIIIIIIIIII

I n 2006, after two years of retirement, Jay-Z made his return as a rapper. His return may have been business related. As a rapper, he could bolster sales for Def Jam, where he was still the CEO. But coming out of retirement may have had more to do with his love for making rhymes. These rhymes kept coming to him, and eventually he decided to once again let them out on stage and in the studio.

That year, Jay-Z released the album *Kingdom Come*, but it did not sell as well as his other albums. In 2007, Jay-Z stepped down as CEO of Def Jam and became a full-time rapper once again. Between Jay-Z's retirement and comeback, the hip-hop world had expanded. Rap music may have first developed in the inner-city areas of the United States, but, as Jay-Z saw firsthand, it had made its way to radios across the Atlantic Ocean.

||||||||||||||||||||||||||||||||||||||||||||||||||||||||

## A WELCOME GUEST

The Glastonbury Festival in England is one of the biggest outdoor musical festivals in the world. In 2008, Jay-Z was invited to perform there. Noel Gallagher, the lead guitarist for the British

## WORKING HARD IN HIS COMEBACK

When Jay-Z decided to come back to rapping in 2006, he produced two albums in a year. The first was *Kingdom Come*. The second was *American Gangster* (2007). His inspiration for the second album was the movie with the same name. In the movie, Denzel Washington plays 1970s Harlem gangster Frank Lucas. Jay-Z used Lucas as an analogy for his own life as a hustler. He was so inspired by the movie that he made the album in a few weeks.

Throughout its history, hip-hop has rubbed some people the wrong way. One objection to the genre is the amount of boasting in rap songs. Jay-Z says boastful rapping should be understood as a genre of hip-hop, just as a sonnet is a genre of poetry. In a sonnet, a writer is required to write in a certain meter and for a certain number of lines. These restrictions mean that a sonnet writer has to work hard to come up with new ways of talking about the same subjects, such as love, and still sound fresh. Similarly, when a rapper boasts in his or her song, he or she is forced to come up with new and creative word choices. Otherwise, the claim that he or she is the best rapper will be proven untrue.

music group Oasis, said, "I'm not having hip-hop at Glastonbury. It's wrong."[1] Once again, Jay-Z felt that he and his music were being treated as unwanted guests. But despite Gallagher's outcry, he didn't actually have anything to do with who was or wasn't invited to play at Glastonbury.

Instead of protesting or boycotting the event, Jay-Z performed as planned. Before he appeared on stage, a video played that included Gallagher's quote. Then Jay-Z showed up with a guitar slung around his neck. He began singing "Wonderwall," one of Oasis's hit songs, and the fans loved it.

Jay-Z and Beyoncé married in 2008.

They also loved Jay-Z's own songs. Approximately 180,000 people were at the concert, and they spent the whole time cheering, chanting, and singing along. It turned out that neither Jay-Z nor his music were unwanted after all.

## A WEDDING

By the morning of April 4, 2008, rumors were circulating in the news about Jay-Z and Beyoncé getting married. One headline read, "Beyoncé and Jay-Z Definitely, Maybe Getting Married Today."[2] Another claimed, "We Are Sooooo Not Buying It."[3] Out-of-state family members had been spotted in New York. So had musicians and friends. A giant tent had been pitched on the rooftop of Jay-Z's penthouse. Orchids and candelabras had been delivered to his doorstep.

But if they were getting married, why had Beyoncé's mother been spotted wearing all black? Other questions fueled speculation and continued to swirl until three weeks later, when the couple confirmed that they had, indeed, tied the knot. For six years, the music superstars had been boyfriend and girlfriend. Now they were husband and wife.

## AN IMPORTANT ELECTION

The year 2008 was also a big year in US politics. George W. Bush had served as president for eight years, and a new president would be elected in

November. Jay-Z hoped that this new president would be Illinois senator Barack Obama.

Jay-Z liked the senator's political policies, but even more important, he liked Obama's biography. Before going to Harvard Law School, Obama had worked as a community organizer in the south side of Chicago. In doing so, he likely met kids growing up in circumstances similar to Jay-Z's childhood. Jay-Z believed that electing an African-American president of the United States would forever change the way African-American kids viewed themselves. "[Obama] could," Jay-Z said, "through sheer symbolism, regardless of any of his actual policies, change the lives of millions of black kids who now saw something different to aspire to."[4]

|||||||||||||||||||||||||||||||||||||||||||||||||||

## A NEW SENSE OF HOPE, THE SAME BUSINESS SENSE

Jay-Z was also busy doing business in 2008. He signed a ten-year, $150 million deal with Live Nation, one of the world's biggest producers of live concerts. Together, Live Nation and Jay-Z created a new all-encompassing entertainment company called Roc Nation. The company is involved in

Jay-Z was an active supporter of Obama in the 2008 presidential election.

every aspect of its clients' work. It represents not only singers and songwriters, but also producers and music engineers. It participates in the promotion of tours and the selling of merchandise, tickets, and even movie rights. Roc Nation aims to do for other musicians many of the things Jay-Z was already doing for his own music.

Jay-Z will likely continue performing well into the future.

## WHAT'S NEXT?

Hip-hop is full of contradictions. Throughout its history it has been viewed as violent, sexist, and materialistic. On the other hand, hip-hop has told a narrative about urban life that otherwise might not have been told. It has given a voice to people who otherwise felt voiceless. Hip-hop can be crude, but it can also be poetic. Jay-Z's music has reflected both of these aspects. He freely admits that he has both done and rapped about bad things, but he has also given back to others in need.

Jay-Z has displayed amazing staying power. His linguistic talent and musical skill have made him a top-selling rapper. As a businessman, he has owned or presided over clothing lines, clubs, record labels, production companies, and sports teams. But the man who has mastered so many different roles in music, business, and life has at least one more to go: fatherhood. On August 28, 2011, after singing a song at the MTV Video Music Awards, Beyoncé rubbed her pregnant belly to show her growing baby bump. The crowd roared its applause as TV cameras panned to Jay-Z in the front row. Jay-Z, the man who was once a scrawny kid with a talent for rhyming, looked like he was on top of the world.

||||||||||

# TIMELINE

## 1969
Shawn Corey Carter is born on December 4.

## 1980
Jay-Z's father, Adnis Reeves, leaves the family.

## 1984
Jaz-O becomes Jay-Z's rap mentor.

## mid-1990s
Jay-Z begins recording *Reasonable Doubt*.

## 1995
Jay-Z founds record label Roc-A-Fella Records with Damon Dash.

## 1996
Jay-Z's first album, *Reasonable Doubt*, is released in June by Freeze Records and Priority Records.

| 1980s | 1988 | 1989 |
|-------|------|------|

Jay-Z quits high school.

Jay-Z tours in London, England, with Jaz-O.

Jay-Z joins Big Daddy Kane's bus tour.

| 1997 | 1998 | 1999 |
|------|------|------|

Jay-Z's second album, *In My Lifetime, Vol. 1*, is released.

Jay-Z's third album, *Vol. 2 . . . Hard Knock Life*, is released.

Jay-Z and Dash start their own clothing line, Rocawear.

# TIMELINE

## 2002
Jay-Z collaborates with Beyoncé Knowles on the song "03 Bonnie and Clyde."

## 2003
Jay-Z founds the Shawn Carter Scholarship Foundation.

## 2003
Jay-Z releases his eighth album, *The Black Album*, on November 14.

## 2005
Jay-Z becomes the CEO of Def Jam Records.

## 2006
Jay-Z works with the United Nations to make the documentary *Water for Life*.

## 2006
Jay-Z returns to rap and releases his ninth album, *Kingdom Come*.

**2003**

Jay-Z retires from rap on November 25.

**2003**

Jay-Z reunites with his father shortly before his father dies.

**2004**

Jay-Z becomes co-owner of the New Jersey Nets.

**2007**

Jay-Z releases his tenth album, *American Gangster*.

**2008**

Jay-Z marries Beyoncé.

**2011**

On August 28, Beyoncé announces she and Jay-Z are expecting their first child.

## FULL NAME

Shawn Corey Carter

## DATE OF BIRTH

December 4, 1969

## PLACE OF BIRTH

Brooklyn, New York

## SELECTED ALBUMS

*Reasonable Doubt* (1996), *In My Lifetime, Vol. 1* (1997), *Vol. 2 . . . Hard Knock Life* (1998), *The Black Album* (2003), *Kingdom Come* (2006), *American Gangster* (2007)

## AWARDS AND HONORS

- One of the most prolific and successful rappers in history, Jay-Z released his first eight albums in eight years, selling millions of records.
- As of 2011, Jay-Z has won nine Grammy Awards in categories including Best Rap Album, Best Rap/Sung Collaboration, and Best Rap Solo Performance.

## BUSINESS

- Jay-Z founded the record label Roc-A-Fella Records with Damon Dash in 1995.

- Jay-Z began the successful clothing company Rocawear in 1999.

- In 2003, Jay-Z opened the nightclub 40/40 in New York City.

- In 2004, Jay-Z became a co-owner of the New Jersey Nets.

- Jay-Z was CEO of Def Jam Records from 2005 to 2007, where he signed artists such as Rihanna and Nas.

## PHILANTHROPY

- In 2003, Jay-Z founded the Shawn Carter Scholarship Foundation. The foundation's goal is to provide underprivileged kids with the opportunity to attend college.

- In 2006, Jay-Z teamed up with the United Nations to make a documentary called *Water for Life* about water scarcity in Africa.

- Jay-Z donated $1 million to the Red Cross for Hurricane Katrina relief.

**"The world wants to think [that] people are drawn to violence [in songs] but when you live in the ghetto you see violence all the time, so that's not the real excitement. If they want to see violence, all they have to do is go home."**

*—JAY-Z*

# GLOSSARY

**battle**—An onstage showdown between two rappers in which the crowd determines the winner.

**choreographed**—Arranged the specific movements and steps for a dance.

**collaborate**—To work together in order to create or produce a work, such as a song or an album.

**diamond**—A certification for an album that has sold 10 million copies.

**finale**—The end of a show or performance.

**freestyle**—To perform verses on the spot rather than from prewritten lyrics.

**Grammy Award**—One of several awards the National Academy of Recording Arts and Sciences presents each year to honor musical achievement.

**hip-hop**—A style of popular music associated with US urban culture that features rap spoken against a background of electronic music or beats.

**hustler**—A slang term for a drug dealer.

**icon**—A person viewed as a representative or symbol of something.

**mogul**—Someone who has achieved tremendous wealth.

**persona**—A popular hip-hop device in which the rapper takes on a voice and personality that isn't actually his or her own.

**producer**—Someone who oversees or provides money for a play, television show, movie, or album.

**rap**—A musical genre composed of rhythmic talking, often accompanied by a beat.

**record label**—A brand or trademark related to the marketing of music videos and recordings.

**single**—An individual song that is distributed on its own over the radio and other mediums.

**studio**—A room with electronic recording equipment where music is recorded.

**track**—A portion of a recording containing a single song or a piece of music.

# ADDITIONAL RESOURCES

## SELECTED BIBLIOGRAPHY

Chang, Jeff. *Can't Stop, Won't Stop: A History of the Hip-Hop Generation*. New York: St. Martin's, 2005. Print.

Greenburg, Zack O'Malley. *Empire State of Mind*. New York: Portfolio/Penguin, 2011. Print.

Jay-Z. *Decoded*. New York: Spiegal and Grau, 2010. Print.

## FURTHER READINGS

Burns, Kate, ed. *Rap Music and Culture*. Detroit, MI: Greenhaven, 2008. Print.

Dyson, Michael Eric. *Know What I Mean? Reflections on Hip-Hop*. New York: Basic Civitas Books, 2007. Print.

## WEB SITES

To learn more about Jay-Z, visit ABDO Publishing Company online at **www.abdopublishing.com**. Web sites about Jay-Z are featured on our Book Links page. These links are routinely monitored and updated to provide the most current information available.

## PLACES TO VISIT

### The Grammy Museum
800 W. Olympic Boulevard, Los Angeles, CA 90015-1300
213-765-6800
http://www.grammymuseum.org
The Grammy Museum features exhibits related to many
genres of music.

### Yankee Stadium
1 East 161st Street, Bronx, NY 10451-2100
646-977-8400
http://www.newyork.yankees.mlb.com/nyy/ballpark/index.jsp
Jay-Z's favorite baseball team plays its home games at this
stadium. Jay-Z is often in attendance.

# SOURCE NOTES

## CHAPTER 1. FAMOUS NEW YORKER

1. Andrea Peyser. "Adoring Fans Do Jeterian Swoon." *New York Post*. NYP Holdings, 7 Nov. 2009. Web. 20 Oct. 2011.

2. Gabe Pressman, et. al. "Run This Town: New York in a Yankees States of Mind." *NBC New York*. NBCUniversal, 6 Nov. 2009. Web. 20 Oct. 2011.

3. "At Yankee Stadium, Jay-Z Doesn't Alter His Line." *New York Times*. New York Times Company, 29 Oct. 2009. Web. 20 Oct. 2011.

4. Zack O'Malley Greenburg. *Empire State of Mind*. New York: Portfolio/Penguin, 2011. Print. 52.

## CHAPTER 2. GROWING UP

None.

## CHAPTER 3. THE ROAD TO RAP

1. Zack O'Malley Greenburg. *Empire State of Mind*. New York: Portfolio/Penguin, 2011. Print. 15.

2. Ibid. 16–17.

3. "Oprah Talks to Jay-Z." *Oprah.com*. Harpo Productions, n.d. Web. 20 Oct. 2011.

4. Jay-Z. *Decoded*. New York: Spiegal and Grau, 2010. Print. 17.

5. Zack O'Malley Greenburg. *Empire State of Mind*. New York: Portfolio/Penguin, 2011. Print. 19.

## CHAPTER 4. MORE RAPPING AND DEALING

None.

## CHAPTER 5. CONVINCING THE REASONABLE DOUBTERS

1. Zack O'Malley Greenburg. *Empire State of Mind*. New York: Portfolio/Penguin, 2011. Print. 33–34.

2. Michael A. Gonzales. "Jay Z: On Racism, Violence & the N Word." *Hip Hop Cosign*. N.p., 17 Dec. 2001. Web. 20 Oct. 2011.

3. "Jay-Z Interview on Centerstage Part 2." *YouTube*. YouTube, 17 Feb 2010. Web. 20 Oct. 2011.

## CHAPTER 6. MORE MUSIC

1. "Jay-Z Interview on Centerstage Part 2." *YouTube*. YouTube, 17 Feb 2010. Web. 20 Oct. 2011.

2. Zack O'Malley Greenburg. *Empire State of Mind*. New York: Portfolio/Penguin, 2011. Print. 40.

3. "100 Best Albums of the Nineties." *Rolling Stone*. Rolling Stone, n.d. Web. 20 Oct. 2011.

## CHAPTER 7. CRIME AND RELATIONSHIPS

1. Jay-Z. *Decoded*. New York: Spiegal and Grau, 2010. Print. 113.

2. Ibid. 120.

3. Zack O'Malley Greenburg. *Empire State of Mind*. New York: Portfolio/Penguin, 2011. Print. 144.

## CHAPTER 8. RETIREMENT AND GETTING HIRED

1. Zack O'Malley Greenburg. *Empire State of Mind*. New York: Portfolio/Penguin, 2011. Print. 83–84.

2. Jay-Z. *Decoded*. New York: Spiegal and Grau, 2010. Print. 249.

3. "Jay-Z's 40/40 Club and Delaware North Companies Announce Airport Partnership." New York: 40/40 Club, 30 Nov. 2010. Web. 20 Oct. 2011.

## CHAPTER 9. GIVING BACK

1. "Oprah Talks to Jay-Z." *Oprah.com*. Harpo Productions, n.d. Web. 20 Oct. 2011.

2. Ibid.

3. Jay-Z. *Decoded*. New York: Spiegal and Grau, 2010. Print. 219

# CHAPTER 10. LOOKING TOWARD THE FUTURE

1. Jay-Z. *Decoded.* New York: Spiegal and Grau, 2010. Print. 163.

2. Zack O'Malley Greenburg. *Empire State of Mind.* New York: Portfolio/Penguin, 2011. Print. 135–137.

3. Ibid. 135–137.

4. Jay-Z. *Decoded.* New York: Spiegal and Grau, 2010. Print. 168.

# ABOUT THE AUTHOR

Paul Hoblin has a master of fine arts in creative writing from the University of Minnesota. He has written several books for children.

# PHOTO CREDITS